Bible Nuggets
from A to Z

by Amber Bennett

Christian Liberty Press

A publication of
Christian Liberty Press
502 West Euclid Avenue
Arlington Heights, Illinois 60004
www.christianlibertypress.com

Author: Amber Bennett
Cover art and Illustrations: David Bergquist
Editor: Edward Shewan
Copyediting: Diane C. Olson
Design: Bob Fine

Scripture references are conformed to The Holy Bible, New King James Version © 1982, Thomas Nelson, Inc., so that modern readers may gain greater comprehension of the Word of God.

CHRISTIAN LIBERTY PRESS
502 West Euclid Avenue
Arlington Heights, Illinois 60004
www.christianlibertypress.com

ISBN: 978-1-932971-71-2

Printed in the United States of America

Contents

Contents (cont.)

Introduction

Bible Nuggets from A to Z provides thirty-four Bible lessons. Each lesson is designed to be taught for an entire week. One Bible story should be read every day for a week. As your child becomes more familiar with the story as the week goes on, begin to ask the questions that are provided at the end of each story.

A Bible verse for memorization is provided with each week's Bible story. Instructors are encouraged to use as many hand motions as possible when memorizing these verses, as hand motions give the student something physical to connect to the words. If you wish to learn some sign language to use with the verses, a good website to use is **aslpro.com**. Scroll down to the "**Religious Dictionary.**"

As students continue to hear each Bible story and verse multiple times, they should become quite familiar with both by the end of each week.

This Bible story book follows an A to Z format. It begins with two lessons that explain the power of the Lord Jesus Christ. These first two lessons emphasize who the Lord Jesus is. Lessons three and following take on an A to Z format, beginning with A is for Adam. Lessons 14 and 25 leave the A to Z format for one week each in order to emphasize the Christmas and Easter stories, respectively. Therefore, lesson thirty is Z is for Zacchaeus. The final four lessons were chosen to emphasize obedience to parents, obedience to God, God's love for little children, and God's power and plan for His people.

Teacher hints are provided in the yellow box at the end of each lesson. The companion *Bible Nuggets Activity Book* includes crafts and activities that will help children remember the lesson.

Although this Bible story book does stand alone, it also works well with the rest of Christian Liberty's preschool program materials. This book is designed to complement the Christian Liberty Preschool program.

Dedication

To Mom and Dad,
for teaching me the truth.

Lesson One

Jesus Tells the Storm to Stop

Matthew 8:23–27

One day, Jesus and His disciples got into a boat. They took the boat out into the sea because they wanted to get to the other side of the sea. While they were in the boat, Jesus fell asleep. While Jesus was sleeping, a huge storm came up. Waves were crashing over the boat, and the wind was blowing very strongly. The disciples were afraid. They woke Jesus up and asked Him to save them. They thought they were going to die.

Jesus asked His disciples, "Why are you fearful, O you of little faith?" Then Jesus stood up and told the wind and the sea to be quiet. The wind and the sea obeyed, and the storm stopped. There was a great calm over the sea.

Jesus' disciples were amazed. They asked each other, "Who can this be, that even the winds and the sea obey Him?"

Memory Verse

Even the winds and the sea obey Him.
-Matthew 8:27b

Questions:

1) What was Jesus doing when the storm came?

2) What did the disciples think was going to happen to them?

3) What did Jesus say to the winds and the waves?

Lesson One: Jesus Tells the Storm to Stop

Emphasize that Jesus is the Lord of all creation. Everything in creation obeys Jesus, even the winds and the seas. The disciples saw the power of Jesus when He told the wind and the sea to obey Him. Jesus Christ is in control of the whole world.

4

Lesson Two

Feeding the Five Thousand

Mark 6:33–44, John 6:1–13

Jesus was often followed by large crowds of people. One day, when Jesus saw a large crowd waiting for Him, He felt sorry for them. He knew that they were lost, like sheep without a shepherd. They needed to be taught. So He stopped to teach them.

Soon the whole day was gone, and the people were still there. There were five thousand people listening to Jesus. The people were hungry because there was nowhere to get food where Jesus was teaching. Jesus' disciples did not have food for all those people. Because it was so late, the disciples wanted to send the people away so that they could all find food. But Jesus told the disciples to give the people food.

The disciples were not sure what to do, but Jesus asked how much food they had. Jesus' disciple Andrew answered that the only food there belonged to a little boy. The boy had five loaves of bread and two fish. This was not enough food for all of the people, but the boy gave his food to Jesus anyway.

Jesus had the people sit down. Then He took the food, and He thanked the Father for it. Then He gave the food to the people, and all the people ate as much food as they wanted. When the people were done eating, Jesus told His disciples to gather up what was left of the food. The disciples gathered twelve baskets of leftover food.

Memory Verse

For He cares for you.
I Peter 5:7b

Questions:

1) How many people were listening to Jesus?

2) Who shared his lunch with Jesus and the people?

3) How many baskets of food were left over?

Lesson Two: Feeding the Five Thousand

Emphasize sharing. The little boy shared his food with Jesus, and Jesus made one small boy's food into enough food for five thousand people. Jesus fed the people this way because He cared about them. He knew that they were hungry, so He provided enough food for all of them. He also thanked His Father for the food. Talk about thanking God for everything He gives us.

Lesson Three

Adam and Eve

Genesis 2 and 3

Adam was the first man that God created. God made Adam out of the dust and breathed life into him. God gave Adam the Garden of Eden to live in. The garden was full of beautiful trees, plants, and animals. When God first created Adam, He gave Adam a very special job. God told Adam to name all of the animals. God brought every animal to Adam so that he could name them all. Adam did a good job.

But Adam did not find a helper for himself among the animals. God wanted Adam to have a helper, so He made Adam fall deeply asleep. He took one of Adam's ribs and made a woman. Adam called the first woman, his wife, Eve. Together, Adam and Eve were supposed to take care of the Garden of Eden. They were happy in the garden.

Adam and Eve were allowed to eat the fruit of any tree that grew in the garden except for the fruit from the Tree of the Knowledge of Good and Evil. God told them not to eat the fruit from that tree. But there was a snake in the garden who was very sneaky. One day, the snake came and asked Eve if God had really told her not to eat from the Tree of Knowledge. Eve said that yes, God had told them not to eat from that tree or they would die. The snake told Eve that if she ate the fruit, she would not die but would become like God and know the difference between good and evil.

Eve saw that the fruit looked good to eat. She took some of the fruit that God had forbidden and ate it. She also gave some to Adam. As soon as Adam and Eve ate the fruit, they knew that they had sinned; this means they disobeyed God's command. God knew it too. Even though Adam tried to say the sin was Eve's fault, and Eve tried to say the sin was the snake's fault, God knew that Adam and Eve had both sinned. Because of their sin, God made Adam and Eve leave the Garden of Eden. And because of the sin that entered the world that day, life became a lot harder for Adam and Eve.

Memory Verse

As for me and my house, we will serve the Lord.
Joshua 24:15b

Questions:

1) What was Adam made out of?

2) What was the name of the garden where Adam and Eve lived?

3) What animal was very sneaky?

Lesson Three: Adam and Eve

Emphasize the fact that all men are now sinners. God created a perfect world, but because Adam and Eve sinned, all men are now born as sinners. We all do bad things. But God did not leave us in our sin. Instead, He sent His Son to die for the sins of His people. Talk about how Jesus saves people from their sins. If we love God, we need to serve Him. If we serve God, then He will bless us.

8

Best Buddies: David and Jonathan

I Samuel 18:1–4, 20:1–42

Saul was the first human king of God's people Israel. But Saul was a bad king, and God chose a new king to rule His people. The new king's name was David. But David couldn't become king until Saul was gone, and Saul didn't like that God had chosen David to be the new king. David had to run away from Saul because Saul wanted to kill him. He was scared sometimes, and he didn't always have a lot of friends to help him.

But God gave David one very good friend. David's friend was named Jonathan. Jonathan and David loved each other as godly friends should. Jonathan showed his friendship by giving David his robe, armor, sword, bow, and belt.

Now Jonathan was King Saul's son. Jonathan did not like that his dad was chasing David. He knew that God had chosen David to be the next king. When David was scared that Saul was going to kill him, he went to Jonathan. Jonathan tried to stop his dad from being angry with David, but Saul still wanted to kill David. He even got mad at Jonathan

for being David's friend. But Jonathan knew that he had to protect his friend.

Jonathan told David that he had to run or Saul would kill him. Jonathan and David were both very sad. But Jonathan said to David, "Go in peace, since we have both sworn in the name of the LORD, saying, 'May the LORD be between you and me, and between your descendants and my descendants, forever.'" David and Jonathan were best buddies. They were friends who honored and obeyed God.

Memory Verse

Believe on the Lord Jesus Christ.
Acts 16:31b

Questions:

1) Who was David's friend and Saul's son?

2) Why did Saul want to kill David?

3) How did Jonathan save David from Saul?

Lesson Four: Best Buddies: David and Jonathan

Emphasize godly friendship. David and Jonathan were good friends. They honored God with their friendship, just like we should. David and Jonathan believed God's promise that David would become king. They believed that God would do what was right, even when they didn't understand everything that was happening. Talk about trusting in God in every situation in life.

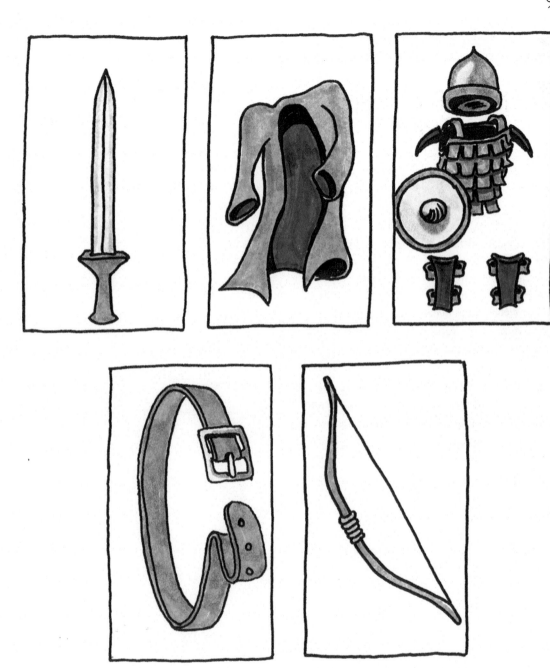

Calling the Disciples: Jesus' Helpers

Matthew 4:18–25, 9:9–13, 10:1–15

When Jesus grew up, He began to go through Israel to teach and heal the people. He knew that He would need some special helpers. Jesus chose twelve men to stay with Him and learn from Him. These men were very special to Jesus, and He needed them to listen and obey Him.

Jesus told these men to stop whatever they were doing and to follow Him instead. They all obeyed. The first two men were brothers, Simon Peter and Andrew. Then Jesus called another set of brothers, James and John. All four of these men were fishermen. Jesus called them from their boats.

Later, Jesus called Matthew, who collected taxes from the people. The other men's names were Philip, Bartholomew, Thomas, James the son of Alphaeus, Thaddaeus, and Simon the Canaanite. The last man was Judas Iscariot. Judas Iscariot was chosen with the other eleven, but he was a wicked disciple. He did not love Jesus. He betrayed Jesus to the soldiers who wanted to kill Jesus. But the other eleven men obeyed Jesus and helped Him.

These twelve men were called Jesus' disciples. While Jesus was on earth, He taught these men about Himself. When Jesus died, rose again, and went to heaven, He sent the disciples all over the world to teach other people about Jesus. The eleven disciples who loved and obeyed Jesus were good helpers, and the Lord blessed them.

Memory Verse

Casting all your care upon Him, for He cares for you.

I Peter 5:7

Questions:

1) How many men did Jesus call to be His helpers?

2) What did Jesus call His helpers?

3) What was the name of the wicked disciple?

Lesson Five: Calling the Disciples: Jesus' Helpers

Emphasize helping others, particularly Jesus. Jesus called His disciples to be helpers. They obeyed immediately. They left whatever they were doing to follow Him. We need to be obedient helpers too. God has called us to obey Him. He will help us to obey Him just like the eleven good disciples did. And when we have trouble obeying God, we need to ask Him for help. Talk about how, if we tell God all of our problems, He will help us because He cares about us, just as He cared for the disciples.

Lesson Six

David and Goliath

I Samuel 17

David was a boy who was chosen by God. He had been chosen by God to be king of Israel after Saul, but he had also been chosen to lead Israel's army in a special way. This was interesting because David grew up as a shepherd boy, not a soldier. He was often out in the fields, keeping his sheep safe and happy. This little shepherd boy knew how to use a sling to protect his flock.

While David was keeping the sheep, Saul was going into battle against the Philistines. The Philistines were wicked people who didn't believe in God. David's three oldest brothers went with Saul to fight against the Philistines. The Philistines had a giant on their side. The giant's name was Goliath. Two times every day, Goliath would come out of his tent and talk to Saul's army. He wanted one of Saul's men to come and fight him. If Goliath won, he wanted Saul's whole army to give up. If Saul's soldier won, then the Philistines would give up. Goliath made fun of Saul and the Israelites. He said they could never beat him. Saul and his army were scared. They thought Goliath was right; they would never win.

But David knew better. He came to bring food to his brothers and their captain in the army. While he was there, he saw Goliath. David wanted to know what gave this giant the right to speak against the army of the living God. He said that if no one else would fight the giant, then he would. David knew God would help him beat Goliath.

Saul tried to give David his armor to protect him, but David wouldn't take it. The armor was too big, and David knew the only protection he needed would come from God. So David took his sling and five small stones and went to fight the giant. Goliath thought he would win easily. But David said, "The battle is the LORD's," and he threw a stone straight into Goliath's forehead. Then David took Goliath's sword to cut off the giant's head. God's army beat the Philistines.

Memory Verse

Delight yourself also in the LORD.
Psalm 37:4a

Questions:

1) What did David use to protect his flock?

2) What was the giant's name?

3) How many stones did David need to throw at the giant?

Lesson Six: David and Goliath

Emphasize trusting in God. David taught the people to trust in the Lord even when things seemed impossible. David delighted in the Lord and trusted that He would protect him. David beat Goliath through God's power.

Evil Repaid: Samson the Strong Man

Judges 13–16

Israel was the nation of God. But the Israelites kept doing wicked things. Then God punished His people by letting other nations rule them. Soon Israel asked for God to forgive them, and He did. When God forgave Israel, He sent them a judge to free them from the other nations. One of those judges was Samson.

Manoah and his wife had no children. But God sent an Angel to tell them that they would have a son, and that he would be special. The son's name was Samson. Before he was born, the Angel told Samson's parents not to cut his hair. Samson's long hair was one sign that Samson belonged to God and was obeying Him. When Samson grew up, he was so strong that he could kill a lion with his bare hands.

When Samson was a man, he married a Philistine woman. The Philistines were the people who were ruling Israel. They were not nice people. They cheated Samson and took his wife away. Samson became very angry and killed thirty Philistines. He also took three hundred foxes and tied them together, tail to tail. Then he put torches of fire between the foxes' tails and sent them into the Philistines' fields. The foxes set fire to all the Philistines' fields and burned them down. When the Philistines caught him and tried to tie him up, Samson broke out of the ropes. The Philistines

tried to catch him again, but he escaped from their trap by picking up the entire gate of a city and carrying it away. Samson's strength helped deliver Israel from the Philistines. Samson was very strong, and his strength came from God alone.

But Samson had a problem. He loved a Philistine woman, Delilah, and God didn't like that. Samson knew that he belonged to God and the Philistine woman did not. The Philistines didn't know how to catch Samson because he was so strong. They asked Delilah to ask Samson how to take away his strength. Samson told Delilah that if he cut his hair, then his strength would go away. Delilah got his hair cut, and the Lord's strength left Samson. The Philistines caught Samson, tied him up, and blinded him. Samson was sad, but he asked the Lord to give him strength one more time. God said yes, and Samson pushed down a whole building on top of many Philistines. He set Israel free through God's strength.

Memory Verse

Every knee shall bow to Me, and every tongue shall confess to God.
Romans 14:11b

Questions:

1) Where was Samson's wife from?

2) What kind of animal did Samson use to burn the Philistines' fields?

3) How did Delilah take Samson's strength away?

Lesson Seven: Evil Repaid: Samson the Strong Man

Emphasize obeying God and God's strength. Samson saved God's people through God's power. When he disobeyed God, God took his strength away. God is more powerful than any man. We need to bow down to Him and say that He alone is God. Talk about relying on God's strength and not our own.

Lesson Eight

Fiery Furnace: Shadrach, Meshach, and Abednego

Daniel 3

Israel was in trouble again. They had disobeyed God, and another nation of bad people had come and taken over. Some of Israel's people were taken far away from their homes. They had to go and live in the nation that had captured them. They had to live in Babylon. Three men who had to go live in Babylon were Shadrach, Meshach, and Abednego.

Nebuchadnezzar was the king of Babylon. He set up an idol for all the people of the land to come and worship. He said that anyone who did not worship his idol would be thrown into a fiery furnace and burned to death. Shadrach, Meshach, and Abednego knew that they could worship only God. They did not bow down to the idol. King Nebuchadnezzar was angry, but he gave them a second chance. Still, the three men would not worship anyone or anything except God. Nebuchadnezzar was so angry that he made the fire even hotter. Then he had Shadrach, Meshach, and Abednego thrown into the fire.

The three men should have been burned up. But Nebuchadnezzar looked into the fire and saw some men walking around in the fire. Three of the men were Shadrach, Meshach, and Abednego. But there was a fourth man. Nebuchadnezzar said that the fourth man "is like the Son of God." Nebuchadnezzar told the three men to come out of the fire. Not a single hair on their heads had been touched by the fire. God saved His servants Shadrach, Meshach, and Abednego from the fire.

Memory Verse

For God so loved the world that He gave His only begotten Son, that whoever believes in Him should not perish but have everlasting life.
John 3:16

Questions:

1) Where did Shadrach, Meshach, and Abednego have to live?

2) What did Nebuchadnezzar want all the people to do?

3) What happened when Nebuchadnezzar threw Shadrach, Meshach, and Abednego into the fire?

Lesson Eight: Fiery Furnace: Shadrach, Meshach, and Abednego

Emphasize being faithful to God. Shadrach, Meshach, and Abednego trusted God to save them. They knew that they should only ever worship the true God. They knew that God loved them and that, even if they died in the fire, they would live with Him in heaven. God chose to save them from the fire. Shadrach, Meshach, and Abednego walked out of the fire and continued to live for God. Talk about ways that we can live for God today.

Lesson Nine

God's Guidance: Moses as a Baby

Exodus 2:1–10

Before God gave His people Israel their own land, the people lived in Egypt. The Egyptians did not like the Israelites. They thought there were too many Israelites. They were afraid of the Israelites. So the Egyptian king, called Pharaoh, made the Israelites their slaves. Then he told the Israelites that they could not have any more baby boys. He said that all Israelite baby boys needed to be killed.

One Israelite family did not obey. God gave them a baby boy. Instead of killing him, they hid him for three months. But then the baby was too big to hide any more. The baby's mother made a basket of reeds and put the baby inside. Then she put the basket in the water. The baby's sister watched the basket from the river bank to see what would happen.

Pharaoh's daughter came down to the river to take a bath. She saw the basket and had her maids pull it out of the water. Pharaoh's daughter saw the baby and knew he was an Israelite baby boy. Moses' sister came out of the reeds she was hiding behind and talked to Pharaoh's daughter. Pharaoh's daughter decided to let the baby's sister find someone to care for the baby until he was old enough to live with her in the palace. The baby's sister went and found her mother.

The baby's real mother took care of him until he was old enough to live with Pharaoh's daughter in the palace. When the baby was old enough, his mother brought him to live in the palace. Pharaoh's daughter named the little boy Moses. He grew up in the palace of Egypt, but he was still an Israelite. God would use this special baby to bring His people out of Egypt and into their own land.

Memory Verse

Give thanks to the LORD.

1 Chronicles 16:8a

Questions:

1) What did the Pharaoh want to do to all the Israelites' baby boys?

2) Where did Moses' mother put him when he was too big to hide?

3) Who found baby Moses?

Lesson Nine: God's Guidance: Moses as a Baby

Emphasize God's guidance in life. God saved Moses from death when he was a baby. He gave Moses a family that would protect and care for him. When his real family couldn't take care of him anymore, God gave Moses an Egyptian family to take care of him.

God showed mercy to Moses by letting him live. He was also preparing Moses for the special job he was going to have to do. Moses would need God's guidance through his whole life.

Helping Others: The Good Samaritan

Luke 10:25–37

A parable is a story that helps people understand something that can be hard to understand. Jesus told a lot of parables to help teach the people who listened to Him. One of those parables was the story of the Good Samaritan. Jesus told this story when someone asked Him how he could get eternal life. Jesus told him to love the Lord with all his heart, soul, and mind. He also said to love his neighbor as himself. Then Jesus explained with this story what a neighbor is.

Once, there was a man who was going on a trip. But some thieves came and stole everything from him, hurt him, and left him to die. The man could not even get up to find help.

Now a priest was traveling along the same road. He saw the hurt man, but he ignored him. He walked past on the other side of the road. Next came a Levite. This man also saw the hurt man but ignored him. He walked right past on the other side of the road. Finally, a third man came down the road. The third man was a Samaritan. He saw the hurt man and stopped to help. The Samaritan bandaged the hurt man's wounds and brought him to a place where he could care for him.

Jesus was explaining that every man we meet is our neighbor. When we see someone who needs our help, we should not ignore him. We should help him. Jesus told the people to be like the Samaritan who helped the hurt man.

Memory Verse

My Hope is in You.

Psalm 39:7b

Questions:

1) What happened to the man who was traveling on the road?

2) What did the first two men who came do for the hurt man?

3) What kind of man was the man who stopped to help?

Lesson Ten: Helping Others: The Good Samaritan

Emphasize helping other people. Note that Jesus was telling His story to Jews. The Jews did not like the Samaritans. But in Jesus' story, the Jewish priest and Jewish Levite walked right past the hurt man. The Samaritan stopped to help. Talk about helping whoever needs our help, not just the people we like. That is obeying God's command to love our neighbor.

22

Lesson Eleven

In a Manger: The Story of Jesus' Birth

Matthew 1, Luke 1:26–56, 2:1–7

Mary was the mother of Jesus. She was going to get married to a man named Joseph. But before they were married, the angel Gabriel told her that she was going to have a baby who was God's Son. Mary was to name the baby Jesus. Mary was afraid, but she praised the Lord for His miraculous work.

Then the angel went to Joseph and told him that he could still take Mary as his wife. The angel told Joseph that Mary's baby was from the Holy Spirit and that He would save His people from their sins. Joseph obeyed the angel and took Mary as his wife.

When it was almost time for the baby to be born, the ruler of the country said that everyone had to go to their home town to be counted. So Joseph and Mary had to travel to Bethlehem. While they were in Bethlehem, it was time for Mary to have her baby. Joseph and Mary had tried to find a place to stay in Bethlehem, but there was no room for them in any of the inns. Instead, they had to stay in a stable. The stable was where Mary had her baby. When He was born, she wrapped Him in swaddling clothes and laid Him in a manger. They named the baby Jesus.

Memory Verse

Glory to God In the highest, and on earth peace, goodwill toward men!
Luke 2:14

Questions:

1) Who was Jesus' mother?

2) Who was going to marry Jesus' mother?

3) Where was baby Jesus born?

Lesson Eleven: In a Manger: The Story of Jesus' Birth

Emphasize that Jesus was both God and man. He came to earth as a baby to save His people from their sins. He was born in a tiny town called Bethlehem, and He was placed in a manger for a bed. But this tiny little baby was still God's Son. He was born for a very special purpose. Only Jesus could save His people from their sin. Talk about how Jesus came to earth just to save His people because He loved them.

Lesson Twelve

Jesus' Birth: The Shepherds and the Angels

Luke 2:8–20

On the night that Jesus was born, there were some shepherds nearby. These shepherds were living in fields and watching their sheep. It was night, when suddenly an angel stood before them. The glory of the Lord shone around them. The shepherds were afraid.

The angel told the shepherds not to be afraid. The angel had news that would be a great joy for all people. The angel told them about Jesus. He said, "For there is born to you this day in the city of David a Savior, who is Christ the Lord." He told them they would find the baby wrapped in swaddling clothes and lying in a manger. Then many more angels appeared. They all said together, "Glory to God in the highest, and on earth peace, goodwill toward men!"

After the angels went back to heaven, the shepherds wanted to go and find the baby. They went to Bethlehem and found Mary and Joseph. And the baby Jesus was there too, lying in the manger. Then they went and told a lot of people what they had seen. Everyone was amazed by what the shepherds had seen.

Then the shepherds went back to their sheep, glorifying God. They praised Him for everything they had seen and heard that night.

Memory Verse

Make a Joyful shout to God, all the earth!

Psalm 66:1

Questions:

1) How did the shepherds feel when they saw the angels?

2) What did the angels tell the shepherds?

3) What did the shepherds do after they found baby Jesus?

Lesson Twelve: Jesus' Birth: The Shepherds and the Angels

Emphasize God's glory. God wanted a lot of people to know that His Son had been born on earth. He sent His angels to tell the shepherds. The shepherds were afraid, but when they learned why the angels were there, they were excited. They knew that God's Son had been born. They gave God the glory for sending His Son to earth to save His people from sin.

Lesson Thirteen

King Jesus: The Wise Men Visit Jesus

Matthew 2

After Jesus was born, wise men came from the East. They asked where the King of the Jews had been born. The King of the Jews was Jesus. The wise men said they had seen the King's star in the night sky. They had followed His star all the way to Jerusalem. They wanted to worship King Jesus.

At this time, Herod was king of Jerusalem. He did not want another king to be born. Herod found out that Jesus was in Bethlehem. He told the wise men to go and find Him. He asked them to tell him when they found Jesus. He said he wanted to worship Jesus, too, but he really wanted to kill Jesus.

The wise men left Herod and kept following the star. The star led them to where Jesus was. They went inside and saw Mary and Jesus. The wise men worshiped Jesus. Then they gave Him gifts of gold, frankincense, and myrrh.

Before they left, God warned the wise men not to tell Herod where Jesus was. So the wise men left without talking to Herod. But Herod was angry. He still wanted Jesus to be killed. He wanted to be the only king. Herod had all the baby boys, two years old and younger, killed.

But Jesus was saved because an angel told Joseph in a dream to take Mary and Jesus and to run away. Mary, Joseph, and Jesus went to Egypt. When Herod died, Joseph had another dream in which an angel told him it was safe to take his family back to Israel. God protected Jesus. Herod could not kill Him because Jesus was and is the King of all kings.

Memory Verse

For He is Lord of lords and King of Kings

Revelation 17:14b

Questions:

1) Where did the wise men come from?

2) What presents did the wise men give to Jesus?

3) Where did the angel tell Joseph to take Jesus to keep Him safe?

Lesson Thirteen: King Jesus: The Wise Men Visit Jesus

Emphasize that Jesus is the King of kings. Note that the wise men were important people in their country. But they understood how much more important Jesus was. They came from far away to worship Him and to give Him gifts. Herod wanted to be the only king, but Jesus is the real King. Jesus is the King of all kings. God protected His Son on earth. No one can rule over God.

Lesson Fourteen

John the Baptist

Luke 1

Once there was a man named Zacharias. He was a priest. His wife's name was Elizabeth. They had no children, even though they were getting old. While Zacharias was serving as a priest, he went into the temple to worship God. While he was in the temple, an angel appeared. The angel told him he and Elizabeth would have a son. He said to name their son John. John was going to be a very special man. He was going to prepare the way for Jesus, the Son of God.

Zacharias was not sure if he believed the angel. He knew he and his wife were old. He didn't think they could have a child. Because he didn't believe, the angel told Zacharias he would not be able to talk until the baby was born. When he came out of the temple, all the people were amazed because he could no longer talk.

What the angel said was true. Zacharias and Elizabeth had a son. When he was born, the people around them wanted to name him Zacharias after his father. But Zacharias remembered what the angel said. He wrote down that the baby's name

was John. As soon as he wrote that, Zacharias was able to talk again. He spoke and praised God.

The hand of the Lord was with John. He became known as John the Baptist. He lived in the wilderness and ate locusts and honey. He was only a few months older than Jesus, the Son of God. He told all the people who would listen about Jesus. He told them that Jesus was coming to save His people from their sins.

Memory Verse

Blessed is the Lord God of Israel, For He has visited and redeemed His people.

Luke 1:68

Questions:

1) What was Zacharias supposed to name his son?

2) What was Zacharias not allowed to do until John was born?

3) What did John eat when he lived in the wilderness?

Lesson Fourteen: John the Baptist

Emphasize God's provision for His people. God wanted His people to hear about His Son, and He used John to tell them. Zacharias knew that his son was going to be very special. John had the very special job of telling all the people in Israel that the Son of God was coming and that they should listen to and worship Him. He knew that Jesus was the only way to salvation.

Lesson Fifteen

Daniel in the Lions' Den

Daniel 6

Daniel was a man who honored God. He was an Israelite who had been taken from his home. For many years he lived in a faraway country. Now he was living under people who were called the Medes and the Persians. God helped Daniel no matter where he lived.

Darius was the king of the Medes and Persians. He had a lot of governors and people to help him rule. Daniel was one of the helpers, and Darius liked Daniel. He even thought about letting Daniel be in control of his whole kingdom.

Darius' other helpers were jealous of Daniel. They didn't want him to rule over them. They tried to find Daniel doing something wrong so they could tell the king. But the only thing they found out about Daniel was that he was faithful to God. Daniel was so faithful that he prayed three times a day to God. The other helpers decided to get Daniel in trouble because he prayed to God.

They told King Darius that he should make a new law. The law would say that no one could pray to anyone except Darius for thirty days. Whoever disobeyed would be thrown into a den of lions. Darius said that he liked the idea. So the new law

was made. Daniel did not stop praying to God. He prayed three times a day like he always did. Darius' other helpers were watching. They went and told the king that Daniel had disobeyed.

King Darius was very upset. He did not want to put Daniel in the lions' den. But he had made the law. So Daniel was thrown into the lions' den. Before he threw Daniel in, Darius said that Daniel's God would save him from the lions. And he was right. When men came the next morning, Daniel was alive. God had sent an angel to shut the lions' mouths. They could not eat Daniel. King Darius was glad that Daniel was alive. He took Daniel out of the lions' den. Then he threw his other bad helpers into the lions' den. Darius told all his people to worship God instead of him.

Memory Verse

Let us Love one another, for Love is of God.

I John 4:7a

Questions:

1) What was the name of the king who liked Daniel?

2) What did Daniel do three times a day?

3) What happened to the bad helpers at the end of the story?

Lesson Fifteen: Daniel in the Lions' Den

Emphasize praying to God at all times. Daniel was a good helper because he obeyed God. Even when the king made a bad law, Daniel obeyed God. He prayed to God. And God saved him from the lions. Talk about how God protects the people who obey Him.

Moses and the Burning Bush

Exodus 2:11–3:22

When Moses, the baby in the basket, grew up, he went to see his own people, the Israelites. The Israelites were still slaves. Moses saw one Egyptian beating an Israelite. Moses killed the Egyptian. When the Pharaoh found out, he wanted to kill Moses. But Moses ran away.

Moses lived in a new land for a long time. He lived as a shepherd. One day, while Moses was with the sheep, he saw a strange bush. There was fire in the bush, but the bush was not burning. Moses went to look closer, and God called to him from the bush. He told Moses to take off his sandals because he was on holy ground. Moses hid his face. He knew that God was speaking to him from the fire, and he was afraid to look at God.

God told Moses that the Israelites were still slaves. They were being treated very badly. God had chosen Moses to lead the people out of slavery. Moses did not think he was the right man to do the job. God knew He had picked the right man. God would be with Moses as he went down to Egypt and told the Pharaoh to let God's people go. The job would not be easy. But God would help Moses.

Memory Verse

Wash Me, and I shall be whiter than snow.

Psalm 51:7b

Questions:

1) Why did Moses have to run away from Egypt?

2) What did Moses do for a living after he left Egypt?

3) Why did Moses have to take off his sandals?

Lesson Sixteen: Moses and the Burning Bush

Emphasize God's holiness. God chose Moses for a very special job. When God appeared to Moses, Moses had to take his shoes off. Even the ground around God was holy. Talk about what it means to be holy and what it means to have a holy God.

Naomi and Ruth

Book of Ruth

Once there was a famine in the land of Israel. There was no food for the people to eat. One woman and her family moved to a place called Moab to find food. The woman's name was Naomi. Naomi had two sons. While the family was in Moab, both sons got married. But then Naomi's husband and both of her sons died. Naomi was left alone with her daughters-in-law.

Naomi decided to go back to Israel. Both daughters-in-law said they would come with her. Naomi said they did not have to come. One daughter-in-law went home. But the other one, named Ruth, stayed. Ruth said she would follow Naomi wherever she went and would live with her and worship her God.

When Ruth and Naomi got back to Israel, they had very little food. Ruth went into a neighbor's field to pick up some leftover grain. The neighbor's name was Boaz, and he liked Ruth. Boaz started leaving extra grain for Ruth to pick up. Naomi saw what was happening and told Ruth to go and talk to Boaz. Boaz and Ruth were married. Then they had a son. God had blessed Ruth and Naomi with a new family.

Memory Verse

Now thanks be to God who always leads us in triumph in Christ.

II Corinthians 2:14

Questions:

1) Why did Naomi and her family leave Israel?

2) Who was the only person who stayed with Naomi when she went back to Israel?

3) Who did Ruth marry?

Lesson Seventeen: Naomi and Ruth

Emphasize God's restoration. Naomi had a sad life. She left the land that God had given her people. Her husband and sons all died. But she returned to the land of her God. Ruth came with her. Together, they lived in God's land. God blessed Naomi with a new family when she returned to His land.

Lesson Eighteen

Learning to Obey: The Lost Sheep

Luke 15:1–7

Jesus was sitting with some men one day. These men were upset with Jesus because He spent a lot of time with sinners. Jesus told these men a story to explain why He spent so much time with sinners.

Once there was a man who had one hundred sheep. One day, one of the sheep got lost. The shepherd left the other ninety-nine sheep to look for the one lost sheep. The shepherd searched until he finally found the lost sheep. When he found it, the shepherd was very happy. He carried the sheep home on his shoulders. When he got home, he called his neighbors and told them to be happy too. The shepherd wanted all his friends to rejoice over the lost sheep who had been found.

Jesus told the men that the lost sheep was like a sinner. A sinner is lost and needs to be found. The sinner needs to learn to obey God. And when a sinner that Jesus spends time with repents from his sin and obeys God, then Jesus rejoices.

Memory Verse

The LORD our God we will serve, and His voice we will Obey!

Joshua 24:24b

Questions:

1) Why were some men upset with Jesus?

2) How many sheep did the shepherd have?

3) What did the shepherd do when he found his lost sheep?

Lesson Eighteen: Learning to Obey: The Lost Sheep

Emphasize the fact that Jesus came to save sinners. The men that Jesus was with thought they were too good to spend time with sinners. They thought Jesus should do the same thing. But Jesus knew that the sinners were the ones that needed Him the most. So He spent a lot of time talking to sinners and teaching them. He taught them to obey God. The men Jesus was with needed to learn to obey God too, but they did not understand that. Talk about how Jesus' message was for all sinners.

START HERE

Lesson Nineteen

Paul and Silas in Prison

Acts 16:20–34

Paul and Silas were men who served Jesus. They traveled to many different places to tell people about Jesus. But some people did not like to hear about Jesus. In a place called Macedonia, some men got mad at Paul and Silas for being servants of God. They had Paul and Silas beaten. Then Paul and Silas were put into prison. The jailer put chains on them so they could not escape.

At midnight that night, Paul and Silas were praying and singing in prison. The other prisoners listened to them. While they were praying and singing, there was an earthquake. The whole prison shook, and all of the prison doors were opened and all the prisoners' chains fell off.

The jailer woke up and saw what had happened. He thought all his prisoners had run away, and he was very scared. But Paul called out to him. He told the jailer not to worry. All the prisoners were still there. The jailer was very surprised. He asked Paul and Silas how he could be saved. They told him to believe on the Lord Jesus Christ and he would be saved. Paul and Silas told the jailer and his family all about Jesus. The jailer and his whole family believed. Then the jailer brought Paul and Silas to his own house and fed them. They were all rejoicing over what God had done.

Memory Verse

Pray without ceasing.

I Thessalonians 5:17

Questions:

1) Why were Paul and Silas in prison?

2) What did Paul and Silas do in prison?

3) What did God send that made all the prisoners' chains fall off?

Lesson Nineteen: Paul and Silas in Prison

Emphasize obeying God and praising Him even in hard situations. Paul and Silas told people about Jesus even though some bad men didn't want them to. And even when they were put in prison they did not stop praising Jesus. They kept praying and singing to God. God sent an earthquake to free them. Still, Paul and Silas stayed so they could tell the jailer about Jesus. Paul and Silas were faithful to God even when things got very hard.

Lesson Twenty

Queen Esther

Book of Esther

Esther was a Jewish woman who lived with her cousin Mordecai. At that time, the Jews lived under a king who was not Jewish. The king had a party one day. The king told his wife, the queen, to come to his party. The queen said no. The king became very angry and decided that he wanted a new queen.

The king had all the most beautiful women of the kingdom come to him. He would decide which woman was the best. The woman he chose would be the new queen. Esther was one of the women that were called to come see the king. The king loved Esther more than all the other women. The king made Esther his queen.

The problem was that no one knew that Esther was a Jew, one of God's people. There was an evil man named Haman who wanted to kill all the Jews. Haman talked to the king and the king listened. They set a day for all the Jews to be killed. Esther was sad because she did not want her people to be killed. But she was afraid also.

Esther's cousin Mordecai told Esther that she had been placed in a position to help the Jews. He wanted her to go and ask the king to not kill the Jews. Esther was not supposed to go see the king unless he called her. If he had not called her and she came to see him, the king could decide to kill her. But Esther went anyway. She knew she had to try to save the Jews. The king saw Esther, and he decided she could come talk to him. Esther told the king she wanted to have dinner with him and Haman. The king agreed.

At dinner, the king asked Esther what she wanted. She asked for him and Haman to come have dinner with her again. The king agreed. At the second dinner, Esther told the king what she wanted. She said she wanted her people to live. The king said that her people could live. Then he asked who was trying to kill them. Esther told the king that Haman was trying to kill all of her people. The king was very angry. He had Haman killed. Then he gave Esther and Mordecai Haman's house. Then he said that the Jews were not to be killed. The Jews could defend themselves from anyone who wanted to kill them. Esther and the Jews lived and were very happy.

Memory Verse

A gentle and Quiet spirit, which is very precious in the sight of God

I Peter 3:4

Questions:

1) Which woman did the king love best?

2) Who wanted to kill all the Jews?

3) What did the king do when Esther told him what Haman wanted to do?

Lesson Twenty: Queen Esther

Emphasize how God provides for His people. God helped Esther become queen so that she could help her people the Jews. Esther loved her Jewish people. She wanted them to live. God gave Esther the courage to go and talk to the king. He also helped the king understand that he should not kill the Jews. Esther was beautiful, but more importantly, she followed God and did what was right.

Lesson Twenty-one

Rainbow: Noah's Ark

Genesis 6–9:17

After Adam and Eve sinned, all men and women after them were sinners, too. A while after Adam and Eve died, the people on earth sinned a lot. God saw how wicked the people were and decided to destroy them. He destroyed all the wicked people of the earth. Only one man was saved with his family. That man's name was Noah.

Noah was a righteous man who listened to God. God was going to send a huge flood on the whole earth to kill all the wicked people. He told Noah to build a giant boat called an ark. Noah and his family would live through the flood by staying on the ark. Noah obeyed God and built the ark, even though all the other people made fun of him. The other people did not believe God would send a flood.

Noah and his sons built the ark. Then they took two of every kind of animal and put all of them in the ark. Then Noah and his wife went into the ark. Their sons, Shem, Ham, and Japheth, and their sons' wives came too. When the eight people and all the animals were on the ark, God closed the door. Then God made it rain for forty days. Water covered the whole earth. All the wicked people who did not get on the ark died.

After many days, the water began to go down. The ark landed on a mountain. Noah sent a dove out of the ark. The dove found nowhere to land, so she came back to the ark. When Noah sent the dove out seven days later, she came back with an olive branch in her beak. The water was drying up. Seven days later, the dove was sent out and did not come back. She had found a place to live. Then Noah and his family and all the other animals came out of the ark. God had kept them safe.

When they were on the ground, Noah worshiped God. He offered sacrifices to Him. God was pleased. He promised never to destroy the whole earth with a flood again. He showed Noah a sign of His promise: the rainbow. Noah saw the rainbow and believed God would keep His promise.

Memory Verse

Rejoice in the Lord always. Again I will say, rejoice!
Philippians 4:4

Questions:

1) What did God use to destroy the whole earth?

2) How many people were saved from the flood in the ark?

3) What did God put in the sky to show His promise?

Lesson Twenty-one: Rainbow: Noah's Ark

Emphasize God's promise to save His people. The people on the earth were so wicked that God had to destroy them all—all except Noah. God saved Noah and his family because they obeyed Him. When the flood was over, Noah rejoiced that God had saved him, his family, and the animals. When the rainbow appeared, Noah knew that God would keep His promise. Talk about how God saves and protects the people who obey Him and rejoice in Him.

Lesson Twenty-two

God Saves: Joseph

Genesis 37, 39–45

Once there was a man named Jacob. Jacob had twelve sons. But Jacob loved his son Joseph more than he loved the other sons. Jacob gave Joseph a special coat made of many different colors. Joseph's brothers were jealous. One day, the brothers were out with the sheep. Jacob sent Joseph to see how the brothers were doing. The brothers wanted to kill Joseph. They grabbed him and threw him into a pit. But when slave traders came by, they decided to sell Joseph to them. The slave traders took Joseph far away to Egypt. His brothers took his many-colored coat, dipped it in blood, and showed it to their father. Jacob thought that Joseph was dead.

In Egypt, Joseph worked for a man named Potiphar. Joseph was a good worker. But Potiphar's wife was evil. She had Joseph thrown into jail for something he didn't do. But God was with Joseph, even in prison.

The king of Egypt was called a pharaoh. God sent two men from the pharaoh's house down to the prison. Joseph interpreted dreams for both of those men. One of the men, a butler, was soon brought back to the pharaoh's house. When the pharaoh himself had a dream, the butler remembered that Joseph had interpreted his dream. The pharaoh called Joseph. Joseph interpreted the pharaoh's dream with God's help. The pharaoh liked Joseph so much that he put Joseph in charge of the whole country. Joseph was second in command.

Joseph helped Egypt save up food because God had told him that a famine was coming. When the famine came and there was no food, Egypt still had food because of Joseph. Lots of people came to Joseph to get food. Joseph's brothers even came to get food. They did not recognize Joseph. But Joseph knew them. When he finally told his brothers who he was, they were very scared. They thought he would hate them because of what they had done. But Joseph forgave his brothers. He told them that God had a purpose for him all along. Because of what his brothers did, Joseph was able to save a lot of people. God had a much bigger plan for Joseph than his brothers could have imagined.

Memory Verse

O taste and See that the LORD is good;
Blessed is the man who trusts in Him!
Psalm 34:8

Questions:

1) How many sons did Jacob have?

2) Where was Joseph sent when he was a slave?

3) How did Joseph get out of jail?

Lesson Twenty-two: God saves: Joseph

Emphasize that God has a plan for the lives of His people. Joseph had a hard life. His own brothers sold him as a slave. He had to go to a faraway place, and he was put in jail for something he didn't do. But God was with him through it all. God had a special plan for Joseph. Joseph trusted in God, and God blessed him.

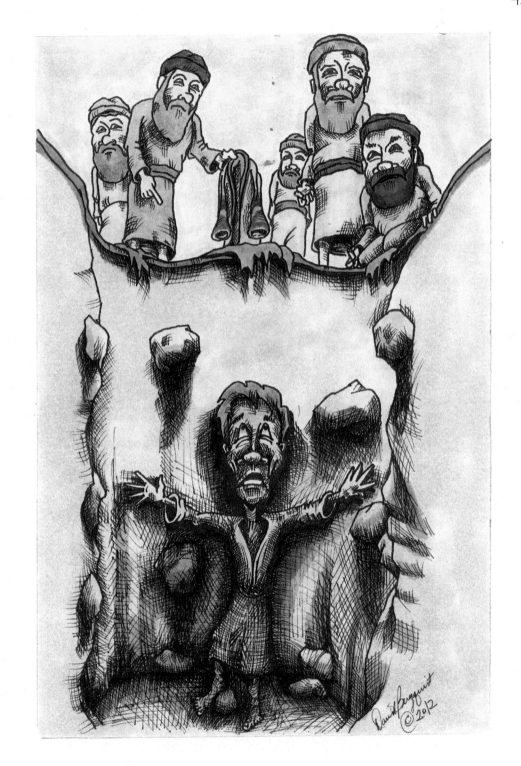

Lesson Twenty-three

Trusting God: Abraham

Genesis 12, 15, 17, 21, 22

Abraham was a man who trusted God. God called Abraham out of his home country. Abraham did not know where he was going. But he obeyed God and started walking. God brought him to a new land and promised to give that land to Abraham's children.

But Abraham did not have any children. He and his wife Sarah were old. They didn't think they could have any children. But God took Abraham out into the night and told him to look at the stars. God promised that Abraham would have as many descendants as there were stars. Abraham believed God.

When Abraham was ninety-nine years old, he still had no children. Sarah was ninety years old. But God still said they would have a child. He promised that He would make Abraham the father of many nations. Abraham and Sarah both laughed, but they still trusted God.

Finally, God's promise came. Abraham and Sarah had a son. They named him Isaac. Abraham loved his son. But God tested Abraham. When Isaac was a young man, God told Abraham to take his son and go up to a mountain. Abraham was supposed to sacrifice Isaac to God. That meant he would have to kill his son. Abraham trusted God. He took Isaac up to the mountain. He prepared the sacrifice. As Abraham was about to kill Isaac, God told him to stop. He told Abraham that there was a ram nearby that Abraham could sacrifice instead. God was happy because Abraham loved God more than anything else, even his son. Abraham trusted that God knew what He was doing. God saved Isaac. His promise to Abraham was true.

Memory Verse

Trust in the LORD with all your heart.

Proverbs 3:5a

Questions:

1) Did Abraham know where he was going when God told him to leave his home?

2) What did God promise to Abraham?

3) What did Abraham name his son?

Lesson Twenty-three: Trusting God: Abraham

Emphasize that God keeps His promises. God called Abraham to trust in Him. Abraham did not know where he was going, but he followed God anyway. He and Sarah were too old to have children, but they believed God would give them a child anyway. Abraham loved Isaac, but he loved God more. He believed that God would somehow protect his son. God kept all of His promises to Abraham.

Lesson Twenty-four

Under the Sea: Jonah

Book of Jonah

God told a man named Jonah to work for Him. He told Jonah to go to a city called Nineveh and warn the people there that God was going to punish them if they kept doing wicked things. Jonah did not want to go. He tried to run away from God.

Jonah got onto a ship that was going away from Nineveh. But God knew where Jonah was. He sent a huge storm over the sea. The boat was in danger of breaking apart. Jonah knew the storm was meant for him. He told the sailors that if they threw him overboard, then the storm would stop. The sailors listened to Jonah. They threw him into the sea, and the storm stopped.

God sent a big fish to where Jonah had been thrown. The fish swallowed Jonah. Jonah stayed in the belly of the fish for three days and three nights. While he was inside the fish, Jonah prayed.

After three days, the fish spit Jonah out onto the dry land. After that, God told Jonah to go to Nineveh. This time, Jonah obeyed.

The city of Nineveh heard Jonah. He told the people to stop doing wicked things. They needed to obey God. The people of Nineveh listened to Jonah. They asked God to forgive them of their sins. God listened and forgave them.

Memory Verse

For Your mercy reaches Unto the heavens.

Psalm 57:10a

Questions:

1) Where did God want Jonah to go?

2) What swallowed Jonah?

3) What did the people of Nineveh do when they heard what Jonah told them?

Lesson Twenty-four: Under the Sea: Jonah

Emphasize the importance of obeying God. Jonah tried to run from God, but God knew exactly where Jonah was. He taught Jonah to listen and obey. Jonah learned to pray to God and to listen to Him. When God gave him a job for the second time, Jonah proved that he had learned his lesson. He listened to God immediately.

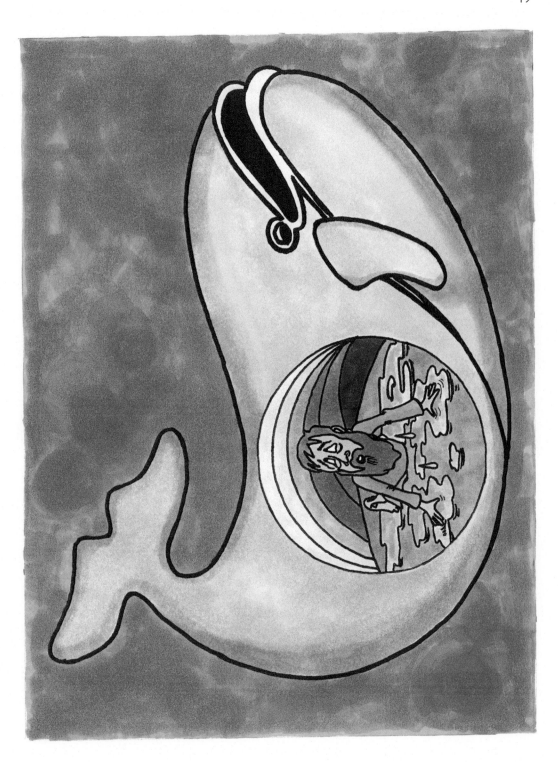

The Easter Story (Crucifixion and Resurrection)

Matthew 27–28, Mark 15–16,
Luke 23–24, John 19–20

When Jesus was on the earth, He knew that He would have to die. His death was the only thing that could save His people from their sin. So after Jesus was done teaching His disciples, He let some people who hated Him take Him away. These people beat Jesus and mocked Him. Then they took Him up to a hill and put Him on a cross to die. Jesus died on the cross that day. Jesus' friends were very sad. They put Him in a tomb and rolled a huge stone in front of the entrance.

Three days later, some women came to put some spices on Jesus' body. But when they got to Jesus' tomb, the stone was rolled away. Jesus was not there. Instead, they saw two angels. The angels told the women that Jesus was no longer dead. Jesus had risen from the dead. He was alive!

The women went to tell the disciples. The disciples had not understood that Jesus would die and then rise again. They did not believe the women. His disciples Peter and John ran to the tomb to see for themselves. When they saw that Jesus was not there, they believed. But they were still confused.

Later, Jesus appeared to all the disciples. He showed them His scars where He had been nailed to the cross. Then the disciples knew for sure that Jesus had been dead but had risen. Jesus stayed with His disciples to help them understand why He had to die and rise again. Then Jesus went up to heaven to be with His Father. The disciples were left on earth to teach others about Jesus and how He died to save His people from their sin.

Memory Verse

He is not here, but is risen!

Luke 24:6a

Questions:

1) What was put in front of Jesus' tomb?

2) How many days was Jesus dead?

3) Did the disciples believe the women who told them Jesus had risen from the dead?

Lesson Twenty-five: The Easter Story

Emphasize that Jesus was dead and rose back to life. He did this willingly to save His people from their sin. All people are sinners. All sin deserves death. No person can save himself from death. Jesus knew that the only way to save His people was to die in their place. He died for His people's sins. But death could not keep Jesus. He defeated death and came back to life. Then He explained everything to His disciples. Now all of Jesus' people know that He paid for our sin so that we do not have to. Someday, if we believe in Jesus, we can live with Him and His Father forever in heaven.

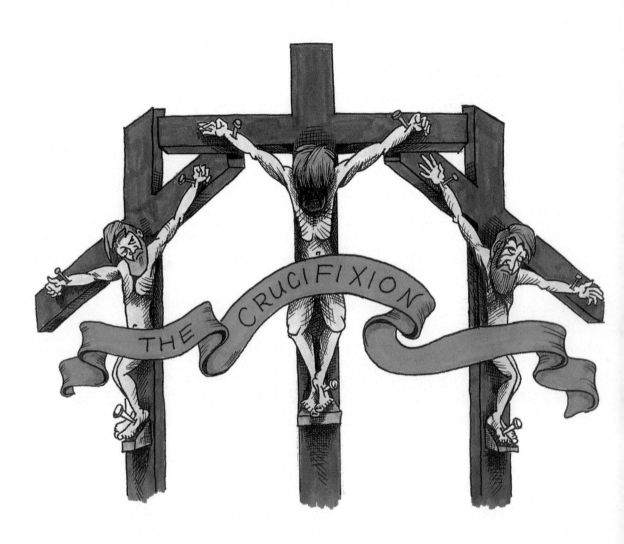

Lesson Twenty-six

Victory in the Lord: Joshua

Joshua 1–6

When God was bringing His people Israel into their new land, He had to choose a new leader for them. He chose Joshua. God told Joshua to be strong and full of courage because he had to lead the people into a new land. The people agreed to follow Joshua.

First, Joshua sent two spies into the new land to see what it was like. The spies were almost captured, but a woman named Rahab saved them. When the spies came back to Joshua, they told him that the land was good. They also said that the people in the land were afraid of Israel's God.

After that, it was time to enter the land. Before they could reach the cities, though, the people had to cross a big river. It was called the Jordan River. God opened the waters of the Jordan River. The people of Israel walked through the middle of the river on dry ground. After that, Joshua and all the people worshiped God.

The city that Israel was going to take over was called Jericho. The people of Jericho shut up their city. They thought Israel could not get through Jericho's big walls. But God told Joshua what to do. Israel marched around the whole city of Jericho once a day for six days. On the seventh day, the people marched around the city seven times. After the seventh time, some people blew horns and they all shouted. When the people shouted, the walls of Jericho fell down. God defeated Jericho for Israel. God was with Joshua and all of Israel.

Memory Verse

The LORD brought about a great
Victory that day.
2 Samuel 23:10b

Questions:

1) Who did God choose to lead the people into their new land?

2) Who saved Joshua's two spies?

3) What happened on the seventh day when the trumpets were blown and the people shouted?

Lesson Twenty-six: Victory in the Lord: Joshua

Emphasize trusting God to win our battles. The Lord chose Joshua to lead the people. When Joshua led the people, he told them what God wanted them to do. God let them cross the river on dry ground, and God made the city walls fall down. Joshua and all the people worshiped God because they knew that it was God who was winning the victory for them. Talk about what the Lord can help you do today and every day.

54

Jesus Walks on Water

Matthew 14:22–33

One evening, Jesus sent His disciples out in a boat. He wanted to spend some time alone, praying to God. While Jesus was praying, His disciples were still in the boat. They were in the middle of the sea, and there was a big wind.

In the middle of the night, Jesus came to the disciples. He walked on the water to reach them. The disciples were afraid. They thought Jesus was a ghost. Jesus told them not to be afraid. He told them who He was.

Jesus' disciple Peter wanted to know for sure that the man he saw was Jesus. He said, "Lord, if it is You, command me to come to You on the water." Jesus told Peter to come. So Peter got out of the boat and started to walk across the water to Jesus. But Peter felt the big wind. He was afraid, and he started to sink. He cried out for Jesus to save him. Jesus grabbed Peter's hand and pulled him up. He asked Peter why he ever doubted that Jesus would keep him safe.

Jesus and Peter got into the boat. As soon as Jesus was in the boat, the wind stopped. Then Jesus' disciples came and worshiped Him. They knew that He was the Son of God.

Memory Verse

Whatever you do, do all to the glory of God.

I Corinthians 10:31b

Questions:

1) What was Jesus doing when His disciples went out in the boat?

2) When Jesus came to them on the water, what did the disciples think He was?

3) What happened to Peter when he stopped trusting Jesus?

Lesson Twenty-seven: Jesus Walks on Water

Emphasize the power of God and our need to trust in Him. Jesus needed to spend some time alone in prayer. But when He went back to the disciples, they were already scared. They did not know who He was. When He told them, Peter needed proof. But when he got out of the boat, he forgot to trust Jesus. That was why he sank. Jesus saved him anyway. He showed all the people in the boat that He really was Jesus, the Son of God. Talk about ways we can see God's power today.

Lesson Twenty-eight

Jesus' EXample: A Pearl of Great Price

Matthew 13:44–46

Jesus knew that His disciples and the other people who listened to Him did not always understand what He was saying. One time, He explained to them how important heaven is. He wanted them to understand that if they wanted to go to heaven, they would have to be willing to give up everything to follow Him. So He told them exactly how important heaven is.

Jesus said that heaven is like a treasure. The treasure had been hidden in a field. One day, a man went out into the field. He found the treasure. He was very excited. The man covered the treasure back up. Then he went and sold everything that he had. With the money he made, he bought the field. The man gave up everything he had to buy that treasure.

Then Jesus said that heaven is also like a merchant who searches for pearls. One day, the merchant found a very wonderful pearl. He sold everything he had and bought that one pearl.

Jesus wanted His disciples to know that heaven is worth everything. The disciples had to be willing to give up everything to get into heaven.

Memory Verse

Christ also suffered for us, leaving us an eXample, that you should follow His steps.

1 Peter 2:21b

Questions:

1) What was Jesus talking about when He told these two stories?

2) What did the man who found a treasure do to make the treasure his?

3) What did the merchant find?

Lesson Twenty-eight: Jesus' Example: A Pearl of Great Price

Emphasize that heaven is where we will live forever with God if we obey and trust in Him. Heaven is worth everything else that we have. Jesus tells us to give up everything for heaven. We can't love anything more than we love Jesus. Talk about how much we should love Jesus.

Lesson Twenty-nine

Yahweh's Garden: Creation

Genesis 1:1–2:3

Yahweh means God. God was the only thing that existed before the world. He created our whole world. A long time ago, there was no earth. There were no stars, animals, or plants. Everything was dark. Then God said, "Let there be light." And there was light. God saw that the light was good. He called the light day. He called the darkness night. That was the first day of creation.

On the second day of creation, God separated the waters. He made the sky. God made dry land on the third day. He called the land earth. He called the water seas. God made trees and plants grow on the earth, as well.

On the fourth day, God made the sun to shine during the day. He made the moon and stars to shine at night. On the fifth day, God created birds and sea creatures. Finally, on the sixth day, God made the animals that live on the land. He also created man in His own image. God made man to rule over the earth.

On the seventh day of creation God rested. He looked at His creation. He knew that it was good. He had created a beautiful world full of wonderful creatures and plants.

Memory Verse

You are all sons of light and sons of the day.

I Thessalonians 5:5a

Questions:

1) What does Yahweh mean?

2) On which day did God create man?

3) What did God do on the seventh day of creation?

Lesson Twenty-nine: Yahweh's Garden: Creation

Emphasize the ability of God to create something out of nothing. Only God can do this. God spent six days creating the world and one day resting from creation. He made Saturday as a day of rest. We need to follow His example.

Talk about why Sunday is now our Sabbath. Explain that since Jesus rose from the dead on Sunday, Christians now worship on that day. Talk about why it is important for us to set that day apart from the rest of the week. Also mention how God made everything perfect and how sin corrupted God's perfect creation.

LIGHT AND DARKNESS

SKY

LAND AND PLANTS

SUN AND MOON

FISH OF THE SEA
BIRDS OF THE SKY

MAN AND WOMAN

60

Lesson Thirty

Zacchaeus

Luke 19:1–9

When Jesus was traveling through Israel, everyone wanted to see Him. The people were curious about this man who could perform miracles. A lot of people wanted Jesus to heal them from sickness. Everywhere Jesus went, there were lots of people.

One time, Jesus was coming into a new town. A lot of people were waiting for Him there. A man named Zacchaeus was there too. But Zacchaeus had a problem. He was too short to see over all the other people. He would not be able to see Jesus when He walked past. So Zacchaeus climbed up into a sycamore tree. When Jesus passed by, He looked up into the tree. He said, "Zacchaeus, make haste and come down, for today I must stay at your house."

Zacchaeus was very happy. He came down from the tree and welcomed Jesus into his home. But the other people who were following Jesus were not happy. They knew that Zacchaeus was a sinner. Zacchaeus was a tax collector. Sometimes he stole money from the people. But Jesus also knew that Zacchaeus was a sinner.

Zacchaeus told Jesus that he would give back four times the amount of money he had stolen. He would also give half of his money to the poor people. Jesus was very pleased. He knew that Zacchaeus did not want to be a sinner anymore. He wanted to follow Jesus. Jesus told Zacchaeus that salvation had come to his house.

Memory Verse

Zacchaeus, make haste and come down, for today I must stay at your house.

Luke 19:5

Questions:

1) Why did all the people want to see Jesus?

2) Why couldn't Zacchaeus see Jesus?

3) What did Zacchaeus say he would do to pay back the money he had stolen?

Lesson Thirty: Zacchaeus

Emphasize that trusting in Jesus is the only way to salvation. Giving away his money to the poor was not enough to save Zacchaeus. His heart had to be in the right place. Jesus knew that Zacchaeus' heart wanted to follow Him. He knew that Zacchaeus was truly saved. Once again, Jesus proved that He needed to spend time with the sinners. The sinners were the ones that Jesus needed to save.

Lesson Thirty-one

Elisha and the Oil

II Kings 4:1–7

Elisha was a great prophet of God. God gave him the ability to perform miracles. One day, a woman came to talk to Elisha. The woman's husband had died. Now the woman owed another man a lot of money. If the woman could not pay, then the man would come and take her two sons away from her. The woman had nothing except a small jar of oil in her house.

Elisha told the woman to gather as many empty pots and jars as she could. When she had done that, she was supposed to pour her jar of oil into the empty pots. The woman agreed to do that. Her sons obeyed her and agreed too. They gathered all the empty pots they could find. Then they went into their house and closed the door. The boys' mother started to pour her oil into the empty pots. The oil did not stop coming. She poured more and more oil into all the empty pots. When she needed another empty jar, her sons brought one to her. Soon, all the empty pots and jars were full. The woman and her sons sold the jars and pots of oil. With the money, they paid their debt. The boys were allowed to stay with their mother.

Memory Verse

Children, obey your parents in the Lord, for this is right.

Ephesians 6:1

Questions:

1) What was the name of God's prophet?

2) Why was a man going to take the woman's sons?

3) What happened to the little jar of oil?

Lesson Thirty-one: Elisha and the Oil

Emphasize obedience. Elisha obeyed God. The woman obeyed Elisha. The boys obeyed their mother. When we learn to obey our parents, we are learning to obey God.

Lesson Thirty-two

The Exodus

Exodus 12:33–50, 13:17–14:31,
16:1–36, 19:1–20:17

Moses was the man God chose to lead His people out of slavery. God used plagues to make Egypt let Israel go. The Egyptians were so afraid of the Israelites that they sent them away with a lot of gold, clothes, and animals. The people of Israel left Egypt with many nice things. They were very happy. They praised God.

Before they got very far, Egypt decided that they did not want to let Israel go. The Egyptians chased the Israelites. The Israelites were scared. They were next to the Red Sea. They couldn't go any farther. But God parted the Red Sea. The Israelites walked across on dry land. When the Egyptians tried to cross, God made all the water go back where it belonged. All of the Egyptians were drowned. God saved Israel from Egypt. And He promised He was going to lead them to a new land that would belong to them. He led them in a pillar of cloud during the day. At night He led them in a pillar of fire.

But the Israelites had a hard time trusting God. They started to complain a lot. They were living in tents in the wilderness. It was a hard life. They complained that they had no food. God heard them, and He sent them special bread from heaven. The bread was called manna. Still, the Israelites complained. God gave them quail to eat and water to drink.

Finally, God led Israel to Mount Sinai. Moses went up the mountain to talk to God. When he came back down, he had laws from God. God told Moses that all people needed to obey those laws. There were a lot of laws, but the main ones were called the Ten Commandments. These laws taught the people how to live. They were to honor God and be kind to their neighbors. God was kind to His people even though they complained that He was not taking care of them.

Memory Verse

You shall love the LORD your God with all your heart, with all your soul, and with all your strength.

Deuteronomy 6:5

Questions:

1) How did God defeat the Egyptians when they chased the Israelites?

2) What did God send down from heaven to feed the Israelites?

3) What did Moses have from God when he came back down the mountain?

Lesson Thirty-two: The Exodus

Emphasize God's love for His people and the law that He wants us to follow. God loved His people and wanted what was best for them. The people did not understand. They wanted more from God. God was taking good care of them, but they still complained. They forgot that God had brought them out of slavery. They were not loving God with all their heart, soul, and strength. But God still took care of them. Talk about how we can obey God's law every day of our lives.

You shall not have any gods before me.

You shall not make any graven images.

You shall not take the Lord's name in vain.

Remember the Sabbath day to keep it holy.

Honor your Father and your Mother.

You shall not kill.

You shall not commit adultery.

You shall not steal.

You shall not bear false witness.

You shall not covet.

Jesus and the Children

Mark 10:13–16

One day, some parents brought their little children to Jesus. They wanted Jesus to bless the children. The disciples did not like this. They thought Jesus had more important things to do than bless children. They thought the children would bother Jesus.

Jesus was not happy with His disciples. He said, "Let the little children come to Me." He wanted the children to come to Him. He told the disciples that the kingdom of heaven was also made for little children. He explained that no one can enter heaven unless he trusts God like a little child.

Then Jesus took the little children in His arms. He laid His hands on them and blessed them.

Memory Verse

Let the little children come to Me.
Mark 10:14b

Questions:

1) Who brought little children to Jesus?

2) What did Jesus say when the disciples tried to make the children go away?

3) What did Jesus do for the children?

Lesson Thirty-three: Jesus and the Children

Emphasize trusting God as a little child. Little children do not doubt and question their parents. They trust their parents. That is how we need to trust Jesus.

Jesus is not just for adults. He loves little children, too, just as little children should love Him.

Jesus said,

"Let the little children come unto me."

Lesson Thirty-four

Peter's Mission

Acts 12:1–19

After Jesus went up to heaven, His disciples were left on earth to tell other people about Him. But a lot of people did not want the disciples to tell people about Jesus. A king named Herod arrested one of Jesus' disciples, James. Herod killed James. Then he arrested another disciple, Peter. He was going to have Peter killed, but God still had a job for Peter.

Peter was kept in prison. He had a lot of guards watching him. But he also had a lot of friends praying for his safety. The night before he was supposed to be killed, Peter was asleep in jail. He was chained to two soldiers who were watching him. More guards were outside. But an angel of the Lord came to Peter. The angel told Peter to get up. The chains fell off Peter's hands.

Peter followed the angel out of the jail. He thought he was dreaming or seeing a vision. The angel took Peter past all the guards. None of the guards noticed their prisoner escaping. The angel took Peter to the gates of the jail. The gates opened all by themselves. The angel led Peter out onto the street. Then the angel disappeared. That was when Peter knew that this was real. The Lord had freed him.

Peter quickly went to where he knew his friends were. They were still praying for him. When he knocked at the house, a girl answered. She was so excited that she forgot to open the door. Instead she ran to find everyone else in the house. The other people did not believe her. But Peter kept knocking until they let him in. All of the people praised God for saving Peter.

Herod was very upset when he found out that Peter was gone. He had had a plan for Peter. But God's plan was bigger. He protected Peter so that Peter could do more work for Him. Peter went on to tell many people about Jesus.

Memory Verse

I will be with him in trouble; I will deliver him and honor him.

Psalm 91:15b

Questions:

1) What did Herod do to James that he also wanted to do to Peter?

2) What happened when Peter came to the gates of the jail?

3) What did the girl who answered the door forget to do?

Lesson Thirty-four: Peter's Mission

Emphasize God's plans and protection for His people. Peter was protected because he loved the Lord and because the Lord had plans for him. The Lord always knows what is best, even if we do not understand. The Lord protects His people from the wicked. The Lord loves those who love Him. He will not let His people be destroyed by the wicked. It was time for James to go home to be with Jesus. But Peter still had a job to do on earth. Talk about what plans Jesus might have for your life.